Jennifer + Chris

On this your wedding day,
May 16, 2009, may all your
tomorrows be as happy as today.
We wish you love and
all the best

Love
Annette + Jack

and they lived happily ever after

pictures and verse
by
Sandra Magsamen

gift

stewart tabori & chang

The secret to a long marriage is to put a little romance into everyday ...

be a best friend and listen to what each other has to say.

Promise
to be fair,
honest, loyal
and
true ...

and give to
each other
understanding
kindness and
thoughtfulness
too.

Share
your dreams
with great
pride ...

treasure
that you have
someone
special with
whom to confide.

Make each other the most important thing in your life . . .

Valuing
each other gives
you joy in
good times and
strength through
the strife.

You won't always agree...

but saying
I am sorry
first after an
argument is
the way it should
be.

Hold
each other
close and
dance under
the stars...

take long
leisurely
rides and
stop to enjoy
ice cream bars.

Walk arm
in arm and
hold each
other
tight ...

and never
forget
to kiss each
other
good night.

Love
each other
with all your
hearts and your
marriage will
be off to a
wonderful start.

Pictures and verse by Sandra Magsamen
© 2000 Hanny Girl Productions, Inc.
Exclusive licensing agent Momentum Partners, Inc., NY, NY

Published in 2000 by
Stewart, Tabori & Chang
A division of U.S. Media Holdings, Inc.
115 West 18th Street
New York, NY 10011

Distributed in Canada by
General Publishing Company Ltd.
30 Lesmill Road
Don Mills, Ontario, Canada M3B 2T6

ISBN: 1-58479-007-5

Printed in Hong Kong

10 9 8 7 6 5 4 3 2 1

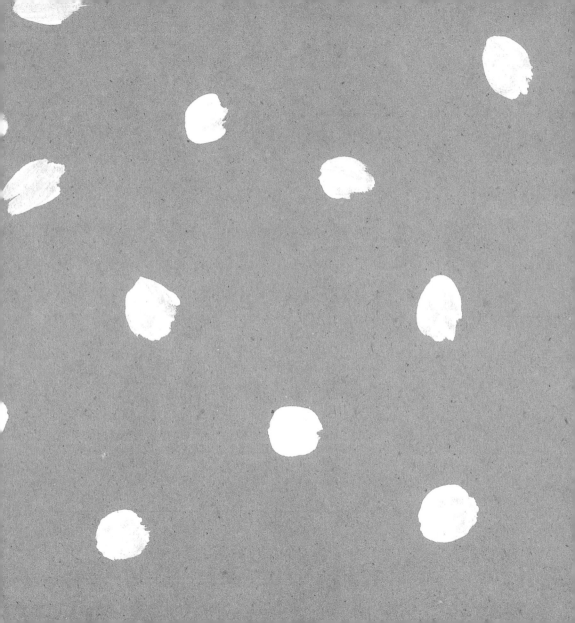